SQUIRREL MONKEY AS PET

A COMPLETE GUIDE TO SQUIIRREL MONKEY HABITAT, CARE, DIET, PROS AND CONS, MANAGEMENT, AND MANY MORE INCLIUDED

DR HUNTER DAVIS

Table of Contents

CHAPTER ONE 5

Introduction..5

CHAPTER TWO 12

Physical Characteristics 12

CHAPTER THREE 23

Habitat and Distribution 23

CHAPTER FOUR 36

Behavior and Social Structure...................................36

CHAPTER FIVE 50

Diet and Feeding Habits...50

CHAPTER SIX 68

Reproduction and Life Cycle.....................................68

CHAPTER SEVEN 86

Predators and Threats 86

CHAPTER EIGHT 103

Interaction with Humans...103

CHAPTER NINE 103

Notable Species 103

CHAPTER TEN 103

Fun Facts and Trivia 103

CHAPTER ONE

Introduction

Overview of Squirrel Monkeys

1.1.1 Taxonomy and Classification

Squirrel monkeys belong to the genus Saimiri within the family Cebidae, which is a part of the New World monkeys. There are several species within the Saimiri genus, with the most well-known being the Common Squirrel Monkey (Saimiri sciureus). Taxonomically, they are classified under the order Primates, which includes other primates like lemurs, tarsiers, and great apes.

1.1.2 Physical Characteristics

Squirrel monkeys are characterized by their small size and distinctive appearance. They typically have a slender body, long tail, and a small, rounded head. Their fur is soft and dense, often displaying vibrant colors such as shades of yellow, orange, and brown. Facial features include large, expressive eyes, a black nose, and a white mask-like marking around their eyes and mouth, giving them a unique and charming expression.

1.1.3 Distribution and Habitat

These monkeys are native to the tropical rainforests of Central and South America, inhabiting a range of environments, including primary and secondary forests. They are highly adaptable and can thrive in various ecosystems, from lowland rainforests to mountainous regions. Squirrel monkeys are known for their agility, enabling them to navigate through the dense vegetation with ease.

1.1.4 Behavior and Social Structure

Squirrel monkeys are diurnal, meaning they are active during the day. They are social animals, forming large groups known as troops. These troops are organized hierarchically, with complex social structures. Within the group, individuals engage in grooming, playing, and vocal communication. Social bonds are crucial for their survival, contributing to cooperative activities such as foraging and predator avoidance.

1.1.5 Diet and Feeding Habits

The diet of squirrel monkeys is omnivorous, consisting of fruits, insects, seeds, and other small invertebrates. They are skilled foragers, using their dexterous hands to manipulate objects and extract food. Their diet plays a vital role in seed dispersal, contributing to the ecological balance of their habitats.

1.1.6 Reproduction and Life Cycle

Mating behaviors among squirrel monkeys involve complex social interactions within the troop. Female squirrel monkeys typically give birth to a single offspring, and the care of the young involves both parents as well as other members of the troop. The infants are carried on the mother's back and are gradually weaned before becoming more independent.

1.1.7 Conservation Status

Squirrel monkeys face various threats, including habitat loss due to deforestation, hunting, and capture for the pet trade. Conservation efforts are crucial to protect their natural habitats and address the challenges posed by human activities. Understanding their behavior, ecology, and the factors impacting their populations is essential for effective conservation initiatives.

In conclusion, the overview of squirrel monkeys encompasses their taxonomy, physical characteristics, distribution, behavior, diet, reproduction, and conservation status. These aspects collectively contribute to a comprehensive understanding of these captivating primates and the importance of their preservation in the wild.

1.2 Taxonomy and Classification

Certainly! The taxonomy and classification of squirrel monkeys provide a systematic framework for understanding their evolutionary relationships and biological categorization. Squirrel monkeys belong to the order Primates, which encompasses a diverse group of mammals that includes lemurs, tarsiers, monkeys, and apes.

1.2 Taxonomy and Classification
1.2.1 Order: Primates

Squirrel monkeys are members of the order Primates, which is characterized by a suite of anatomical and behavioral features associated with adaptation to an arboreal (tree-dwelling) lifestyle. Primates share common traits such as grasping hands and feet, forward-facing eyes, and complex social behaviors. This order is further divided into suborders, infraorders, and families based on more specific characteristics.

1.2.2 Suborder: Haplorhini

Within the order Primates, squirrel monkeys belong to the suborder Haplorhini. This suborder includes tarsiers, monkeys, and apes, and is characterized by dry, non-olfactory rhinarium (the moist, naked surface around the nostrils), relatively larger brain size, and a postorbital plate (bony eye socket closure).

1.2.3 Infraorder: Simiiformes

Squirrel monkeys fall under the infraorder Simiiformes, which comprises two main groups: Platyrrhini (New World monkeys) and Catarrhini (Old World monkeys and apes). Squirrel monkeys are classified under Platyrrhini due to their distinctive flat, outward-facing nostrils.

1.2.4 Family: Cebidae

The family Cebidae includes squirrel monkeys along with other New World monkeys like capuchins and howler monkeys. Members of this family are characterized by a prehensile tail, which means the tail is adapted for grasping objects, aiding in their arboreal lifestyle.

1.2.5 Genus: Saimiri

Squirrel monkeys are further classified into the genus Saimiri. This genus comprises several species, with the most well-known being Saimiri sciureus, commonly known as the Common Squirrel Monkey. The genus name "Saimiri" is derived from a Tupi Indian word.

1.2.6 Species: Saimiri sciureus and Others

The Common Squirrel Monkey (Saimiri sciureus) is just one of the species within the genus Saimiri. Other species include the Black-capped Squirrel Monkey (Saimiri boliviensis) and the Central American Squirrel Monkey (Saimiri oerstedii), among others. Each species may exhibit variations in physical characteristics, distribution, and behavior.

1.2.7 Importance of Classification

Taxonomy and classification are crucial for organizing and understanding the diversity of life on Earth. By categorizing organisms based on shared characteristics, scientists can infer evolutionary relationships and make predictions about the biology and behavior of different species. This information is valuable for conservation efforts, as it helps identify the unique needs and vulnerabilities of specific groups of organisms, including squirrel monkeys.

In conclusion, the taxonomy and classification of squirrel monkeys place them within the broader context of primate diversity, highlighting their evolutionary relationships and distinctive features within the natural world. Understanding their taxonomic placement contributes to our knowledge of their biology, behavior, and ecological roles.

CHAPTER TWO

Physical Characteristics

2.1 Size and Weight

2.1.1 General Physical Characteristics

Squirrel monkeys are relatively small primates with a distinctive appearance. They exhibit sexual dimorphism, meaning there are observable differences between males and females in terms of size and physical features. On average, adult squirrel monkeys have a head and body length ranging from 25 to 35 centimeters (approximately 10 to 14 inches).

2.1.2 Weight Variations

The weight of squirrel monkeys can vary among different species and even within the same species. On average, adult squirrel monkeys weigh between 750 grams to 1.1 kilograms (approximately 1.7 to 2.4 pounds). Females tend to be slightly smaller than males, with a weight range often falling towards the lower end of the spectrum.

2.1.3 Importance of Small Size

The small size of squirrel monkeys is an adaptation to their arboreal lifestyle. Being lightweight allows them to navigate and move easily through the dense vegetation of their natural habitats, primarily tropical rainforests. Their agility in the trees is crucial for foraging, escaping predators, and navigating the complex three-dimensional environment of the forest canopy.

2.1.4 Sexual Dimorphism

Sexual dimorphism in size is more pronounced in squirrel monkeys than in some other primate species. Male squirrel monkeys are generally larger than females. This size difference may be related to social dynamics and reproductive strategies within their group structures. Larger males may have advantages in mate competition or in establishing social dominance within the troop.

2.1.5 Growth and Development

Squirrel monkeys undergo a period of growth and development from birth to adulthood. Newborns are tiny, weighing around 100 grams (approximately 0.22 pounds) and are highly dependent on their mothers for care. As they grow, they become more independent but continue to learn and refine their skills, such as foraging and social behaviors, throughout their lives.

2.1.6 Adaptation to Arboreal Lifestyle

The small size and lightweight build of squirrel monkeys are adaptations to their arboreal habitat. These primates are adept climbers and leapers, using their prehensile tail for balance and their strong limbs for rapid movement through the trees. Their compact size allows them to access a variety of food sources in the canopy, where they find fruits, insects, and other resources.

2.1.7 Ecological Significance

The size and weight of squirrel monkeys have ecological implications. As omnivores, their foraging habits influence seed dispersal in their habitats, contributing to the maintenance of plant diversity. Their small size also makes them vulnerable to predation, emphasizing the importance of their social structures and behaviors for protection against potential threats.

In conclusion, the size and weight of squirrel monkeys are integral to their survival strategies and adaptation to their arboreal habitats. These characteristics influence their behavior, social dynamics, and ecological roles within the intricate ecosystems they inhabit. Understanding their physical traits provides insights into the evolutionary processes that have shaped these captivating primates.

Fur and Coloration

The fur and coloration of squirrel monkeys are distinctive features that play a crucial role in their adaptation to their natural environment, communication within their social groups, and overall survival strategies. Here's an extensive explanation of their fur and coloration:

2.2 Fur and Coloration of Squirrel Monkeys
2.2.1 Fur Texture and Length
Squirrel monkeys are covered in a soft and dense fur that provides insulation and protection in their tropical rainforest habitats. The fur is short to medium in length, contributing to their sleek appearance. The texture of their fur aids in reducing friction as they move through the dense vegetation, allowing for swift and agile movements.

2.2.2 Coloration

One of the most striking features of squirrel monkeys is their vibrant and variable coloration. The color patterns vary among different species and individuals, but some common characteristics include a mixture of colors such as yellow, orange, brown, and black. Their faces often have a distinctive white or pale mask-like pattern around their eyes and mouth, which adds to their expressive appearance.

2.2.3 Camouflage and Concealment

The coloration of squirrel monkeys serves various functions, including camouflage and concealment in their forested habitats. The combination of their fur colors and patterns helps them blend into the dappled sunlight and shadows of the canopy, making it challenging for predators to spot them. This adaptation enhances their chances of avoiding detection and predation.

2.2.4 Social Significance

Coloration also plays a crucial role in social communication within squirrel monkey groups. Individuals within a troop can identify each other based on their unique color patterns. This is particularly important in the context of group cohesion, as it helps maintain social bonds, facilitates cooperation, and reduces the likelihood of aggression between group members.

2.2.5 Temperature Regulation

The fur of squirrel monkeys also plays a role in thermoregulation. In their tropical habitats, temperatures can vary, and the density of their fur helps regulate their body temperature by providing insulation. Additionally, their ability to adjust their fur thickness through piloerection (raising the fur) or flattening it against their bodies aids in temperature control.

2.2.6 Sexual Dimorphism in Coloration

Sexual dimorphism extends to coloration, with males often exhibiting more intense and vivid colors compared to females. The color differences may play a role in mate selection and signaling reproductive fitness. Bright and conspicuous colors in males may serve as indicators of their genetic quality or ability to acquire resources.

2.2.7 Behavioral Significance

The coloration of squirrel monkeys is not only a passive aspect of their appearance but also has active behavioral significance. During social interactions, such as mating displays or confrontations, individuals may use their body colorations and facial expressions to communicate intentions and establish social hierarchies.

2.2.8 Conservation Implications

Changes in fur coloration can be indicative of stress or health issues in squirrel monkeys. Monitoring color patterns and alterations in response to environmental changes or human disturbances can be valuable for assessing the well-being of populations in the wild and informing conservation efforts.

In summary, the fur and coloration of squirrel monkeys are multifaceted adaptations that serve functional roles in their ecology, social dynamics, and survival strategies. These features contribute to their remarkable ability to thrive in the intricate and dynamic environments of tropical rainforests.

Facial Features

The facial features of squirrel monkeys are distinctive and play essential roles in communication, social interactions, and adaptation to their environment. Understanding these facial features provides insights into the behavior, ecology, and evolutionary strategies of these primates.

2.3 Facial Features of Squirrel Monkeys

2.3.1 Mask-Like Coloration

One of the most prominent facial features of squirrel monkeys is the mask-like coloration around their eyes and mouth. This facial pattern typically includes a white or pale area that contrasts with the surrounding fur colors. This feature varies among species and individuals but is a common characteristic in many members of the Saimiri genus.

2.3.2 Eye Structure

Squirrel monkeys have large, forward-facing eyes with well-developed vision. This adaptation is crucial for their arboreal lifestyle, as it helps them navigate through the complex three-dimensional environment of the forest canopy. The size and position of their eyes contribute to depth perception, aiding in activities such as leaping between branches and detecting potential predators or prey.

2.3.3 Nose and Mouth

The nose of squirrel monkeys is typically small and black, and their mouths are adapted for an omnivorous diet. Their teeth include sharp incisors for cutting and tearing food, as well as molars for grinding plant material. The structure of their mouth and teeth reflects their varied diet, which includes fruits, insects, seeds, and other small invertebrates.

2.3.4 Expressive Facial Features

Squirrel monkeys are known for their expressive facial features, and their communication often involves facial expressions. Raised eyebrows, widened eyes, and various mouth movements can convey different emotions and intentions within the social group. These expressions are crucial for maintaining group cohesion, signaling submission or dominance, and facilitating cooperation.

2.3.5 Ear Structure

The ears of squirrel monkeys are relatively small and may not be as prominent as in some other primate species. The ear structure is adapted to their arboreal lifestyle, reducing drag as they move through the forest canopy. While their sense of hearing is important for communication and detecting environmental cues, visual and olfactory senses are also highly developed.

2.3.6 Vibrissae (Whiskers)

Some squirrel monkey species have vibrissae, or whiskers, around their face. These whiskers are sensitive to touch and can aid in navigating through the branches, detecting obstacles, and locating food. While not as prominent as in some other mammals, the presence of vibrissae contributes to their sensory abilities.

2.3.7 Individual Variation

Facial features, including the mask-like coloration, can vary among individuals and species. This variation may have a genetic basis, but environmental factors, such as exposure to sunlight or nutritional status, can also influence the intensity and pattern of facial colors.

2.3.8 Social Significance

Facial features are integral to social interactions within squirrel monkey groups. Recognition of individuals within the troop is facilitated by the unique color patterns and facial characteristics. These features contribute to the establishment of social hierarchies, mate selection, and overall group cohesion.

In conclusion, the facial features of squirrel monkeys are not only distinctive aspects of their appearance but also functional adaptations for their survival in the complex environments of tropical rainforests. The expressive nature of their faces and the unique color patterns contribute to their social dynamics and communication within their groups. Understanding these features enhances our appreciation for the behavioral complexity and evolutionary strategies of squirrel monkeys.

CHAPTER THREE

Habitat and Distribution

3.1 Natural Habitat

The natural habitat of squirrel monkeys is primarily in the tropical rainforests of Central and South America. These habitats are characterized by high temperatures, high humidity, and a rich diversity of plant and animal life. Understanding the natural habitat of squirrel monkeys provides insights into their ecological roles, behavioral adaptations, and the challenges they face in the wild.

3.1.1 Geographic Distribution
Squirrel monkeys are found in a wide range of habitats within Central and South America. Their distribution extends from the isthmus of Panama in Central America through the Amazon Basin and into parts of Brazil, Bolivia, and Peru in South America. Different species may inhabit specific regions within this broad range.

3.1.2 Tropical Rainforests

The primary natural habitat of squirrel monkeys is tropical rainforests, which are characterized by dense vegetation, a variety of tree species, and a complex vertical structure. These monkeys are well-adapted to life in the trees, utilizing the forest canopy for foraging, sleeping, and social interactions.

3.1.3 Arboreal Lifestyle

Squirrel monkeys are highly arboreal, spending the majority of their time in the trees. Their bodies are adapted for climbing, leaping, and moving through the branches with agility. Their prehensile tail is used for balance, and their long limbs allow them to make rapid movements in the canopy, avoiding predators and accessing food resources.

3.1.4 Canopy Living

Within the tropical rainforest, squirrel monkeys predominantly inhabit the canopy layer, which is the uppermost layer of the forest. This region is rich in fruits, leaves, and insects, providing ample food sources for these omnivorous primates. The canopy also offers protection from ground predators and provides a complex three-dimensional environment for navigation.

3.1.5 Biodiversity Hotspots

The natural habitat of squirrel monkeys often overlaps with biodiversity hotspots, regions with exceptionally high levels of species richness and endemism. These hotspots, such as the Amazon Rainforest, are critical for the conservation of global biodiversity. Squirrel monkeys contribute to the intricate ecological web of interactions within these ecosystems.

3.1.6 Microhabitats

While their primary habitat is the tropical rainforest, squirrel monkeys may also utilize different microhabitats within this larger ecosystem. This includes riverine forests, secondary forests, and areas with a mix of forest and savanna. Their adaptability allows them to thrive in various environments, though they are most commonly associated with undisturbed, primary rainforests.

3.1.7 Importance of Water Sources

Water sources are essential components of their habitat. Rivers, streams, and other water bodies within the rainforest provide drinking water and contribute to the availability of food resources. Squirrel monkeys may also use water for bathing and grooming.

3.1.8 Threats to Habitat

The natural habitat of squirrel monkeys faces threats due to human activities such as deforestation, logging, agriculture, and infrastructure development. Habitat loss and fragmentation impact the ability of these monkeys to find food, navigate through the forest, and maintain social structures. Conservation efforts are crucial to mitigate these threats and preserve their natural environment.

In summary, the natural habitat of squirrel monkeys is the tropical rainforest, where they have evolved to thrive in the canopy. Their arboreal lifestyle, adaptability to different microhabitats, and reliance on biodiversity hotspots emphasize the importance of preserving these ecosystems for the well-being of squirrel monkey populations and the broader biodiversity of the region.

3.2 Geographic Range

The geographic range of squirrel monkeys spans across Central and South America, encompassing a variety of ecosystems within the tropical rainforests of the region. Understanding the geographic distribution of squirrel monkeys provides insights into the diversity of species, their ecological preferences, and the conservation challenges they face across their range.

3.2 Geographic Range of Squirrel Monkeys

3.2.1 Central America

In Central America, squirrel monkeys are found in countries such as Panama and parts of Costa Rica and Nicaragua. Their distribution in this region is associated with tropical rainforests and other forested habitats. The Isthmus of Panama serves as a natural barrier, influencing the distribution of various species.

3.2.2 South America

The majority of the geographic range of squirrel monkeys is situated in South America, where they inhabit the vast expanse of the Amazon Rainforest and surrounding areas. Countries within their South American range include Brazil, Peru, Bolivia, Colombia, Ecuador, and Venezuela. Within this expansive territory, different species of squirrel monkeys may have specific ranges and distributions.

3.2.3 Amazon Basin

The Amazon Rainforest, particularly the Amazon Basin, is a critical part of the geographic range of squirrel monkeys. This region is characterized by unparalleled biodiversity and serves as a vital habitat for numerous plant and animal species. Squirrel monkeys play an integral role in the ecological dynamics of this vast and complex ecosystem.

3.2.4 Riverine Forests

Squirrel monkeys are known to inhabit riverine forests, which are ecosystems along riverbanks. These areas provide a mix of terrestrial and aquatic resources, contributing to the overall diversity of their habitat. The proximity to water sources is essential for their hydration and the availability of food resources.

3.2.5 Altitudinal Variation

While squirrel monkeys are primarily associated with lowland tropical rainforests, some species may also inhabit montane or hilly areas. Altitudinal variation in their geographic range allows them to adapt to different environmental conditions, contributing to their ability to occupy diverse habitats within their overall distribution.

3.2.6 Habitat Fragmentation

The geographic range of squirrel monkeys is increasingly affected by habitat fragmentation due to human activities such as logging, agriculture, and infrastructure development. Fragmentation can lead to isolated populations, reducing genetic diversity and making them more vulnerable to environmental changes and threats.

3.2.7 Conservation Challenges

Conservation efforts for squirrel monkeys need to consider the extensive geographic range across multiple countries. Challenges include addressing habitat loss, protecting biodiversity hotspots, and implementing conservation strategies that span political boundaries. Collaborative initiatives involving local communities, governments, and international organizations are crucial for the sustainable management of their habitats.

3.2.8 Climate Change Effects

The geographic range of squirrel monkeys may be influenced by climate change, which can alter the distribution of vegetation and impact food availability. Understanding how these primates respond to changing environmental conditions is important for predicting future range shifts and implementing effective conservation measures.

In summary, the geographic range of squirrel monkeys spans a vast and diverse landscape, primarily within the tropical rainforests of Central and South America. The complexity of their distribution highlights the need for comprehensive conservation strategies that address both local and regional challenges, aiming to safeguard their habitats and ensure the long-term survival of these charismatic primates.

3.3 Habitat Threats and Conservation

The natural habitat of squirrel monkeys faces various threats, primarily driven by human activities. These threats pose significant challenges to the well-being and survival of squirrel monkey populations. Conservation efforts are crucial to mitigate these threats and ensure the preservation of their habitats and overall ecological health.

3.3 Habitat Threats and Conservation
3.3.1 Habitat Loss and Deforestation
Threat:

Deforestation: One of the most significant threats to the habitat of squirrel monkeys is deforestation. Large-scale clearing of land for agriculture, logging, and infrastructure development results in the destruction of their natural habitat. This loss of forest cover directly impacts the availability of resources, disrupts ecological balances, and fragments populations.

Conservation:

Protected Areas: Establishing and expanding protected areas, such as national parks and reserves, is crucial for safeguarding the remaining natural habitats of squirrel monkeys. These areas provide a refuge for wildlife and contribute to the conservation of biodiversity.

3.3.2 Habitat Fragmentation
Threat:

Habitat Fragmentation: Human activities, including the construction of roads and urbanization, lead to habitat fragmentation. This isolates populations of squirrel monkeys, reducing genetic diversity and making them more susceptible to the negative effects of inbreeding.
Conservation:

Corridor Creation: Implementing wildlife corridors that connect fragmented habitats allows for the movement of squirrel monkeys and other wildlife between isolated patches of forest. This helps maintain gene flow and promotes population sustainability.

3.3.3 Agriculture and Plantations
Threat:

Agricultural Expansion: The conversion of natural habitats into agricultural land, including large-scale monoculture plantations, reduces the availability of suitable habitats for squirrel monkeys. Agrochemicals and pesticides used in agriculture can also have detrimental effects on the surrounding ecosystems.
Conservation:

Sustainable Practices: Encouraging and promoting sustainable agricultural practices, such as agroforestry and organic farming, helps minimize the impact on natural habitats. Supporting certifications like Rainforest Alliance can incentivize responsible land use.

3.3.4 Climate Change
Threat:

Climate Change: Climate change poses a threat to the habitat of squirrel monkeys by altering temperature and precipitation patterns, affecting the distribution of vegetation and disrupting ecological processes. Changes in climate can impact the availability of food and water resources.

Conservation:

Climate-Resilient Conservation: Implementing climate-resilient conservation strategies involves adapting to changing environmental conditions. This may include habitat restoration, ensuring water availability, and monitoring the impact of climate change on squirrel monkey populations.

3.3.5 Human-Wildlife Conflict
Threat:

Human-Wildlife Conflict: As human activities encroach upon natural habitats, conflicts between humans and squirrel monkeys may arise. These conflicts can lead to negative perceptions of the species and result in retaliatory killings, further endangering populations.

Conservation:
Community Engagement: Engaging local communities in conservation efforts is vital. Implementing strategies to mitigate human-wildlife conflict, such as the use of deterrents and education programs, helps foster positive relationships between communities and squirrel monkeys.

3.3.6 Poaching and Illegal Trade
Threat:

Poaching and Illegal Trade: Squirrel monkeys are sometimes captured for the illegal pet trade, and their body parts may be used in traditional medicine. Poaching poses a direct threat to individual monkeys and can have cascading effects on populations.

Conservation:

Anti-Poaching Measures: Strengthening anti-poaching measures, improving law enforcement, and increasing public awareness about the consequences of the illegal wildlife trade are crucial for protecting squirrel monkeys from poaching.

3.3.7 Conservation Initiatives

Conservation:

Research and Monitoring: Conducting research on squirrel monkey populations, their behavior, and ecological needs is essential for informed conservation planning. Regular monitoring helps assess the effectiveness of conservation initiatives and adapt strategies as needed.

In summary, addressing the habitat threats faced by squirrel monkeys requires a multi-faceted approach that combines habitat protection, sustainable land-use practices, community engagement, and international cooperation. Conservation efforts should aim not only to protect the habitats of these primates but also to promote the well-being of the entire ecosystems they inhabit.

CHAPTER FOUR

4.1 Diurnal Activities

Squirrel monkeys are diurnal primates, meaning they are primarily active during the daytime. Their diurnal behavior is shaped by various ecological, social, and evolutionary factors. Understanding their diurnal activities provides insights into their daily routines, social interactions, foraging strategies, and adaptations to their natural environment.

4.1.1 Diurnal Adaptations

Being diurnal is an adaptation that allows squirrel monkeys to exploit the daytime environment efficiently. Their visual acuity is well-suited for daylight conditions, and they have color vision, enabling them to discern ripe fruits, detect predators, and navigate through the complex forest canopy.

4.1.2 Social Structure and Group Dynamics

Squirrel monkeys are highly social animals, and their diurnal activities are often centered around group interactions. During the daytime, troop members engage in various social behaviors, including grooming, playing, and vocalizations. These activities strengthen social bonds, establish hierarchies, and contribute to the overall cohesion of the group.

4.1.3 Foraging and Feeding

One of the primary diurnal activities of squirrel monkeys is foraging for food. Their diet is omnivorous and includes fruits, insects, seeds, and other small invertebrates. The daylight hours provide optimal conditions for locating and consuming these food resources, which are abundant in the canopy of tropical rainforests.

Fruit Foraging: Squirrel monkeys are skilled fruit foragers. They use their dexterous hands to manipulate and extract fruits from branches. Their agility allows them to navigate through the canopy, reaching various fruit-bearing trees.

Insect Hunting: In addition to fruits, squirrel monkeys actively hunt for insects. They may capture insects by reaching into tree bark crevices or by chasing them through the foliage. Insect consumption supplements their diet with protein and other nutrients.

4.1.4 Thermoregulation

The daytime environment in tropical rainforests can be warm, and squirrel monkeys engage in thermoregulation to maintain optimal body temperature. They may rest in shaded areas, use their fur to modulate body temperature, and engage in behaviors like panting to cool down if needed.

4.1.5 Predator Avoidance

Being diurnal provides squirrel monkeys with better visibility, allowing them to detect and respond to potential predators. Vigilance and group cohesion help deter predators, and the open canopy of the daytime environment allows for early detection and evasion of threats.

4.1.6 Communication and Vocalizations

Daytime is a crucial period for communication among troop members. Squirrel monkeys use a variety of vocalizations, including calls, whistles, and chirps, to convey information about food sources, alert group members to dangers, and maintain social bonds. These vocalizations contribute to the overall coordination and cohesion of the troop.

4.1.7 Rest and Relaxation

While squirrel monkeys are highly active during the day, they also allocate time for rest and relaxation. Resting periods may involve individuals grooming each other, napping, or simply sitting in a relaxed posture. These moments of repose are important for conserving energy and maintaining overall well-being.

4.1.8 Reproductive Behaviors

Daylight hours are crucial for reproductive behaviors within squirrel monkey troops. Mating, courtship displays, and parenting activities typically occur during the day. The diurnal nature of these activities allows for visual cues, displays, and interactions that contribute to the social and reproductive dynamics of the group.

In conclusion, the diurnal activities of squirrel monkeys are intricately tied to their ecological niche in tropical rainforests. Their adaptation to daylight conditions influences their foraging strategies, social interactions, predator avoidance, and overall survival in the dynamic and diverse environments they inhabit.

4.2 Group Dynamics

Squirrel monkeys exhibit complex and dynamic group dynamics, characterized by social structures, communication, and cooperative behaviors. Understanding these group dynamics is essential for gaining insights into their social organization, reproductive strategies, and responses to environmental challenges.

4.2 Group Dynamics of Squirrel Monkeys

4.2.1 Social Structure

Squirrel monkeys are highly social and live in groups known as troops. These troops can vary in size, typically ranging from 20 to 75 individuals, although larger groups have been observed. The social structure within a troop is organized hierarchically, with individuals occupying different positions based on factors such as age, sex, and social status.

Age and Sex Classes: Within a troop, there are often age and sex classes. Juveniles, subadults, and adults may form distinct groups, and there may be separate male and female hierarchies. Males often compete for dominance and may establish a hierarchy based on size and aggressive displays.

4.2.2 Cooperative Activities

Cooperative behaviors play a crucial role in squirrel monkey group dynamics. Individuals within a troop engage in various cooperative activities that contribute to the overall success and survival of the group. These activities include:

Foraging: Squirrel monkeys forage for food collectively, exploiting the resources of the forest canopy. Cooperative foraging allows them to cover larger areas, share information about food sources, and protect against predators.

Grooming: Grooming is a social activity that strengthens social bonds within the troop. Squirrel monkeys engage in reciprocal grooming, where individuals groom each other, providing not only physical benefits but also reinforcing social relationships.

Predator Avoidance: Living in groups enhances predator avoidance. Cooperative vigilance and alarm calls help alert group members to potential threats. The presence of multiple individuals can deter predators, making it more challenging for them to target a specific individual.

4.2.3 Communication

Communication is a key component of squirrel monkey group dynamics. Vocalizations, facial expressions, body postures, and gestures are used to convey information within the troop. Different vocalizations serve specific purposes, such as signaling danger, coordinating group movements, and maintaining social cohesion.

Alarm Calls: Squirrel monkeys have distinct alarm calls that alert the group to the presence of predators. These calls vary depending on the type of threat, allowing for specific responses from group members.

Affiliative Calls: Affiliative vocalizations are used during social interactions to reinforce social bonds. These calls contribute to the overall cohesion of the troop and help maintain group unity.

4.2.4 Reproductive Strategies

Reproductive behaviors are an integral part of squirrel monkey group dynamics. Mating, courtship displays, and parenting activities occur within the social structure of the troop. The reproductive strategies include:

Mating: Dominant males often have priority in mating, but there may be competition for access to females. Mating can lead to the formation of social bonds between mating pairs.

Parental Care: Squirrel monkeys exhibit cooperative parental care. Both males and females contribute to the care of offspring. Infants are carried on the mother's back, and other group members may participate in grooming and protecting the young.

4.2.5 Social Bonding
Social bonding is crucial for the stability of squirrel monkey troops. Strong social bonds contribute to cooperation, mutual support, and the overall success of the group. Social bonds are reinforced through grooming, affiliative behaviors, and shared activities such as foraging.

4.2.6 Intergroup Interactions

Squirrel monkeys may interact with other troops, and these interactions can range from affiliative to aggressive. Interactions between troops may involve vocalizations, displays, and occasional physical confrontations. The dynamics of intergroup interactions can influence the territoriality and resource access of different troops.

4.2.7 Flexible Group Composition

Squirrel monkey group dynamics can be flexible, with individuals joining or leaving troops. This flexibility allows for changes in group composition based on factors such as social relationships, reproductive opportunities, or environmental conditions.

In conclusion, the group dynamics of squirrel monkeys are characterized by hierarchical social structures, cooperative behaviors, communication strategies, and flexible adaptations to changing conditions. These dynamics enhance their ability to navigate the challenges of their tropical rainforest habitats, contributing to the success and resilience of squirrel monkey populations.

4.3 Communication and Vocalizations

Communication is a vital aspect of squirrel monkey behavior, and vocalizations play a prominent role in conveying information within the troop. Squirrel monkeys utilize a diverse repertoire of vocalizations, each serving specific purposes related to social interactions, predator avoidance, mating, and group cohesion.

4.3 Communication and Vocalizations of Squirrel Monkeys
4.3.1 Types of Vocalizations
Squirrel monkeys produce a wide array of vocalizations, each with distinct acoustic properties and functions. Some of the common types of vocalizations include:

Alarm Calls: Alarm calls are loud, distinctive vocalizations used to alert the troop to potential dangers, such as the presence of predators. Squirrel monkeys are known for having different alarm calls for various types of threats, allowing the troop to respond appropriately.

Contact Calls: Contact calls are soft, high-pitched vocalizations that individuals use to maintain contact with other members of the troop while foraging or moving through the forest. These calls help prevent individuals from becoming separated from the group.

Affiliative Calls: Affiliative vocalizations are used during social interactions to reinforce social bonds. These calls contribute to the overall cohesion of the troop and are often exchanged during grooming or other affiliative behaviors.

Mating Calls: Mating calls are specific vocalizations associated with reproductive behaviors. These calls may play a role in mate attraction and courtship rituals, facilitating communication between potential mates.

4.3.2 Alarm Calls and Predator Recognition
Squirrel monkeys are known for their sophisticated alarm call system, which allows them to communicate specific information about potential threats. The different alarm calls are tailored to indicate the type of predator present, such as aerial predators (birds of prey) or terrestrial threats (mammalian predators). This specificity helps the troop members respond appropriately, whether by seeking cover or adopting defensive postures.

4.3.3 Social Cohesion

Communication through vocalizations is crucial for maintaining social cohesion within the troop. Contact calls, affiliative calls, and other vocal signals contribute to the coordination of group movements, foraging activities, and overall troop unity. The ability to communicate effectively enhances cooperation among group members.

4.3.4 Individual Recognition

Squirrel monkeys are capable of recognizing the individual voices of other troop members. This ability aids in social interactions, as individuals can identify and respond to the calls of specific group members. Individual recognition is important for maintaining social bonds, coordinating activities, and responding to the needs of group members.

4.3.5 Vocal Learning and Flexibility

Squirrel monkeys demonstrate vocal learning, allowing them to adapt their vocalizations based on their social environment. Young monkeys learn vocalizations by listening to and mimicking the calls of older, more experienced individuals. This flexibility in vocal communication contributes to the adaptability of squirrel monkey groups.

4.3.6 Context-Specific Vocalizations

Vocalizations in squirrel monkeys are context-specific, meaning the same type of call may have different meanings depending on the situation. For example, a contact call may serve to maintain group cohesion during foraging, but it can also express distress or separation anxiety if a troop member becomes isolated.

4.3.7 Non-Vocal Communication

While vocalizations are prominent, squirrel monkeys also engage in non-vocal forms of communication. Physical gestures, body postures, and facial expressions are used to convey information about social status, intentions, and emotional states. Non-vocal communication complements vocalizations in the overall communication repertoire of squirrel monkeys.

4.3.8 Environmental Adaptations

Squirrel monkeys have adapted their vocalizations to the environmental conditions of the tropical rainforest. The dense vegetation and complex structure of the forest canopy create acoustic challenges. The unique vocalization system of squirrel monkeys allows them to communicate effectively in this complex auditory environment.

In summary, communication and vocalizations play a critical role in the social dynamics, cooperative behaviors, and overall success of squirrel monkey troops. The diverse array of vocalizations, including alarm calls and affiliative signals, contributes to the complex and adaptive communication system of these highly social primates.

CHAPTER FIVE

Diet and Feeding Habits

5.1 Preferred Food Sources

Squirrel monkeys are omnivorous primates with a varied diet that includes fruits, insects, seeds, and other small invertebrates. Their preferred food sources are influenced by the seasonal availability of resources in their tropical rainforest habitats. Understanding their dietary preferences provides insights into their ecological roles, foraging strategies, and adaptations to their environment.

5.1.1 Fruits

Role in Diet:

Fruits are a major component of the squirrel monkey diet. They provide essential vitamins, minerals, and sugars, contributing to the overall nutritional balance of their diet.

Preferred Fruits:

Squirrel monkeys consume a variety of fruits, including berries, figs, and tropical fruits like bananas and papayas. They are opportunistic feeders, adapting their fruit consumption to the seasonal availability of different fruits in their habitat.

Foraging Strategies:

Squirrel monkeys exhibit agile foraging behaviors, using their prehensile tail and dexterous hands to pluck fruits from branches. They are known for leaping between trees to access a diverse range of fruiting trees in the canopy.

5.1.2 Insects

Role in Diet:

Insects play a crucial role in supplementing the protein content of the squirrel monkey diet. They contribute essential amino acids and micronutrients, enhancing the nutritional diversity of their food sources.

Preferred Insects:

Squirrel monkeys are skilled insect hunters, targeting a variety of invertebrates such as grasshoppers, crickets, caterpillars, and spiders. Their insectivorous behavior is especially prominent during periods when fruit availability is lower.

Foraging Strategies:

Insect foraging involves actively searching for prey in tree bark crevices, leaf litter, and among the branches. Squirrel monkeys may use their hands to catch insects, demonstrating precision and coordination in their hunting techniques.

5.1.3 Seeds and Nuts
Role in Diet:

Seeds and nuts contribute to the squirrel monkey diet, offering a source of fats and carbohydrates. While they may not be as primary as fruits and insects, seeds and nuts become more important during certain times of the year.

Preferred Seeds and Nuts:
Squirrel monkeys may consume seeds from various plant species, including those found in fruits. They may also feed on nuts and seeds directly from tree pods or those dispersed by other animals.

Foraging Strategies:

Foraging for seeds and nuts involves extracting them from the pulpy flesh of fruits or cracking open tougher seed coats to access the edible contents. Squirrel monkeys' manipulative abilities play a role in efficiently extracting and consuming these food items.

5.1.4 Flowers and Plant Parts
Role in Diet:

Certain species of squirrel monkeys include flowers and plant parts in their diet. These items can provide additional nutrients and contribute to dietary diversity.

Preferred Flowers and Plant Parts:

Squirrel monkeys may feed on nectar from flowers or consume other plant parts such as young leaves, buds, and stems. The selection of these plant items depends on species-specific preferences and seasonal availability.

Foraging Strategies:

Foraging for flowers and plant parts involves delicate handling and extraction of nectar or consumption of specific plant structures. Squirrel monkeys may use their hands and mouths to manipulate and access these food items.

5.1.5 Adaptations to Seasonal Changes

Seasonal Variation:

The preferred food sources of squirrel monkeys exhibit seasonal variation. As the availability of fruits, insects, and other food items changes throughout the year, squirrel monkeys adapt their foraging strategies to meet their nutritional needs.

Feeding Flexibility:

Squirrel monkeys demonstrate flexibility in their dietary preferences, adjusting their food choices based on resource availability. This adaptability is essential for their survival in the dynamic and ever-changing environment of the tropical rainforest.

5.1.6 Nutritional Balance

Dietary Diversity:

The omnivorous and opportunistic nature of the squirrel monkey diet allows for a diverse range of food sources. This dietary diversity helps ensure that squirrel monkeys obtain the necessary nutrients for energy, growth, and reproduction.

Balancing Macronutrients:

By incorporating fruits for carbohydrates, insects for protein, and seeds/nuts for fats, squirrel monkeys achieve a balanced macronutrient intake. This nutritional balance supports their physiological needs in the energy-demanding environment of the rainforest.

In summary, squirrel monkeys exhibit dietary preferences for fruits, insects, seeds, and other plant materials, showcasing their adaptability to the seasonal variations in resource availability. Their foraging strategies and diverse food choices contribute to their ecological roles within tropical rainforest ecosystems.

5.2 Foraging Behavior

Squirrel monkeys are highly adaptable and opportunistic foragers, employing a diverse range of behaviors to locate and procure their preferred food sources. Their foraging behavior is influenced by factors such as the seasonal availability of resources, the complex structure of the tropical rainforest, and the social dynamics within the troop.

5.2 Foraging Behavior of Squirrel Monkeys
5.2.1 Arboreal Foraging
Arboreal Lifestyle:

Squirrel monkeys are arboreal primates, spending the majority of their time in the trees. Their foraging behavior is intricately linked to their ability to navigate the complex three-dimensional environment of the forest canopy.

Canopy Exploration:

Foraging primarily takes place in the canopy, where they move skillfully from branch to branch, leaping and climbing to access different levels of the forest. Their long limbs and prehensile tail contribute to their agility in traversing the intricate network of branches.

Efficient Locomotion:

The arboreal lifestyle allows squirrel monkeys to efficiently cover large distances in search of food. They can leap between trees with remarkable precision, avoiding ground predators and accessing a variety of food sources distributed throughout the forest.

5.2.2 Group Foraging
Social Foraging:

Squirrel monkeys are highly social animals, and group foraging is a common behavior within the troop. Foraging as a group provides several advantages, including increased vigilance against predators, the sharing of information about food sources, and cooperative defense against potential threats.

Information Sharing:

Group members communicate about the location of food resources through vocalizations, body language, and observations. This information-sharing helps the troop optimize foraging efficiency and exploit a diverse array of food items.

Coordinated Movement:

Group foraging involves coordinated movements within the troop. Individuals may follow the lead of others to access specific trees or exploit particular feeding sites. This coordination contributes to the overall success of the group in finding and utilizing resources.

5.2.3 Seasonal Variation
Dietary Flexibility:

Squirrel monkeys exhibit dietary flexibility to cope with the seasonal variation in resource availability. As the abundance of fruits, insects, and other food sources changes throughout the year, they adjust their foraging behavior and food preferences accordingly.

Shifts in Foraging Strategies:

During periods of high fruit availability, squirrel monkeys may focus more on fruit foraging, while during times of lower fruit abundance, they may intensify their insect hunting or diversify their diet by incorporating other plant parts.

5.2.4 Tool Use
Manipulative Abilities:

Squirrel monkeys demonstrate manipulative abilities in their foraging behavior. They use their hands and sometimes their mouths to extract insects from tree bark, open seed pods, or manipulate fruits. These manipulative skills are essential for accessing different food items.

Tool Use Instances:

While not as extensively studied as in some other primate species, there are instances where squirrel monkeys have been observed using tools. For example, they may use sticks or other objects to extract insects from crevices or to open hard-shelled fruits.

5.2.5 Gleaning and Pouncing

Gleaning Behavior:

Squirrel monkeys often engage in gleaning behavior, where they carefully inspect leaves, branches, and bark for hidden insects or other small invertebrates. Their keen eyesight and agile movements aid in detecting and capturing prey.

Pouncing Technique:

The pouncing technique involves suddenly leaping or reaching out to grab insects or small prey. This quick and precise movement allows them to catch agile insects or other elusive prey items.

5.2.6 Diet Diversity
Omnivorous Diet:

Squirrel monkeys are omnivores with a diverse diet. Their foraging behavior reflects their ability to exploit a wide range of food sources, including fruits, insects, seeds, flowers, and other plant parts. This omnivorous diet contributes to their adaptability in varying ecological conditions.

Balancing Nutritional Needs:

By diversifying their foraging behavior, squirrel monkeys can balance their nutritional needs, obtaining essential macronutrients and micronutrients from different food sources. This dietary flexibility enhances their resilience in the face of changing environmental conditions.

5.2.7 Learning and Innovation
Social Learning:

Squirrel monkeys engage in social learning, where individuals learn from observing and imitating the foraging behaviors of others within the troop. This social learning contributes to the transmission of efficient foraging techniques and strategies.

Innovation:

In response to changing environmental conditions or the availability of novel food sources, squirrel monkeys may exhibit innovative foraging behaviors. These innovations can spread within the troop through social learning, contributing to the overall adaptive capacity of the group.

In summary, the foraging behavior of squirrel monkeys is a dynamic and adaptive process shaped by their arboreal lifestyle, social dynamics, and the seasonal variation in resource availability. Their ability to diversify their foraging strategies and learn from one another enhances their resilience and success in the tropical rainforest environment.

5.3 Role in Ecosystem

Squirrel monkeys play a significant role in the ecosystems they inhabit, particularly the tropical rainforests of Central and South America. Their presence and activities contribute to the ecological balance and functioning of these diverse and complex environments. Understanding their role in the ecosystem involves examining their impact on vegetation, seed dispersal, predation, and interactions with other species.

5.3 Role of Squirrel Monkeys in the Ecosystem
5.3.1 Seed Dispersal
Consumption and Dispersal:

Squirrel monkeys are important seed dispersers in tropical rainforests. As they feed on fruits, seeds are

often ingested along with the pulp. The seeds pass through their digestive system and are later excreted in different locations, aiding in the dispersal of seeds.
Enhancing Biodiversity:

Seed dispersal by squirrel monkeys contributes to the spatial distribution of plant species within the ecosystem. It helps enhance biodiversity by facilitating the colonization of new areas and promoting genetic diversity within plant populations.

5.3.2 Vegetation Impact
Foraging and Pruning:

Squirrel monkeys engage in active foraging behaviors, including the consumption of leaves, fruits, and other plant parts. While their impact on vegetation is relatively minor compared to larger herbivores, their foraging activities may result in the pruning of branches and selective consumption of certain plant species.

Influence on Plant Growth:

The selective foraging behavior of squirrel monkeys can influence the growth and regeneration of specific plant species. By preferentially consuming certain fruits or leaves, they may indirectly shape the composition and structure of the vegetation in their habitat.

5.3.3 Insect Population Control
Insect Consumption:

Squirrel monkeys are adept insect hunters and consume a variety of invertebrates, including insects. Their foraging activities contribute to the control of insect populations in their environment, helping to regulate the abundance of certain insect species.

Impact on Tree Health:

By feeding on insects that may be harmful to trees, squirrel monkeys indirectly contribute to the health of the vegetation. For example, they may consume insects that feed on tree leaves, mitigating potential damage to the foliage.

5.3.4 Ecological Interactions
Predation Impact:

Squirrel monkeys are themselves prey for various predators, including birds of prey, large snakes, and felids. Their presence and the predation pressure they experience contribute to the intricate web of ecological interactions within their ecosystem.

Predator-Prey Dynamics:

The predation of squirrel monkeys influences the behavior and population dynamics of their predators. For example, the presence of these primates may attract and sustain populations of predators, contributing to the overall balance of predator-prey relationships in the ecosystem.

5.3.5 Ecotourism and Conservation
Economic and Conservation Value:

Squirrel monkeys, being charismatic and easily observed in their natural habitats, contribute to ecotourism. Ecotourism activities centered around observing these primates can generate economic value for local communities and contribute to the conservation of their habitats.

Conservation Awareness:

The presence of squirrel monkeys in ecotourism initiatives can raise awareness about the importance of conserving tropical rainforests and the diverse species that inhabit these ecosystems. Conservation efforts often benefit from increased public awareness and support.

5.3.6 Interactions with Other Species
Synergistic Relationships:

Squirrel monkeys interact with various other species in their ecosystem, forming complex ecological relationships. For example, they may engage in mutualistic relationships with certain plant species that depend on them for seed dispersal, establishing synergistic connections within the ecosystem.

Competition and Coexistence:

Squirrel monkeys may also compete with other frugivores and insectivores for resources such as fruits and insects. Their foraging behaviors and preferences contribute to the dynamics of interspecific competition and coexistence within the ecosystem.

In summary, squirrel monkeys play a multifaceted role in tropical rainforest ecosystems. Their activities influence seed dispersal, vegetation dynamics, insect populations, and contribute to the complex web of ecological interactions. Understanding their role is crucial for appreciating the ecological functions they perform and for developing effective conservation strategies to preserve the biodiversity of their habitats.

CHAPTER SIX

Reproduction and Life Cycle

6.1 Mating Behavior

Squirrel monkeys exhibit complex mating behaviors that are influenced by social structures within the troop, reproductive strategies, and individual interactions. Mating behavior is essential for the continuation of the species, and understanding the intricacies of squirrel monkey mating provides insights into their social dynamics and reproductive success.

6.1.1 Social Structure and Mating Systems
Troop Dynamics:

Squirrel monkeys live in social groups called troops. These troops have hierarchical social structures, with dominant and subordinate individuals. The social structure influences mating dynamics, as dominant individuals often have priority in mating opportunities.

Polygynandrous Mating System:

Squirrel monkeys exhibit a polygynandrous mating system, where both males and females have multiple mating partners within the troop. Dominant males may mate with multiple females, and females may mate with multiple males. This mating system promotes genetic diversity within the troop.

6.1.2 Reproductive Cycles and Estrus
Estrus Cycles:

Female squirrel monkeys typically experience estrus cycles, during which they are sexually receptive and can conceive. The timing of estrus cycles varies among individuals, and females may exhibit behavioral and physical cues signaling their reproductive status.

Mate Choice:

Mate choice is influenced by various factors, including social status, physical condition, and reproductive readiness. Females may preferentially associate with certain males during estrus, and dominant males may have increased access to mating opportunities.

6.1.3 Courtship Displays

Mating Signals:

Squirrel monkeys engage in courtship displays as a means of signaling their reproductive readiness and attracting potential mates. These displays involve a range of behaviors, including vocalizations, facial expressions, body postures, and gestures.

Male Display:

Dominant males may engage in elaborate displays to attract females. These displays can include vocalizations, exaggerated movements, and postures that highlight the male's physical prowess and social status. Courtship displays serve to communicate the male's fitness and suitability as a mate.

6.1.4 Mating Rituals and Copulation
Ritualized Behaviors:

Mating rituals involve ritualized behaviors that precede copulation. These behaviors can include grooming, mutual sniffing, and other affiliative interactions. Rituals serve to strengthen social bonds, reduce tension, and facilitate successful mating.

Copulation:

Copulation in squirrel monkeys occurs between a receptive female and a mating male. The duration and frequency of copulation can vary, and dominant males may have more access to mating opportunities. Copulation is a critical step in the reproductive process, leading to the potential conception of offspring.

6.1.5 Post-Mating Behaviors

Post-Copulatory Displays:

After copulation, both males and females may engage in post-mating displays and behaviors. These behaviors can include grooming, vocalizations, and other affiliative interactions. Post-mating displays contribute to social cohesion within the troop.

Parental Cooperation:

Squirrel monkeys exhibit cooperative parental care, with both males and females contributing to the care of offspring. Post-mating behaviors may involve cooperation between mating partners in caring for and protecting the upcoming offspring.

6.1.6 Male Competition
Dominance Hierarchy:

Male competition for mating opportunities is influenced by the dominance hierarchy within the troop. Dominant males often have priority in accessing estrous females and may engage in aggressive behaviors to maintain their mating status.

Challenges and Competitions:

Challenges between males can include physical confrontations, displays of aggression, and vocalizations. The outcome of these competitions may affect the mating success of individuals within the troop.

6.1.7 Female Choice and Mate Guarding
Female Preferences:

Females may exert mate choice by associating with certain males during estrus. They may prefer males displaying specific traits or behaviors, such as dominance or effective courtship displays.

Mate Guarding:

Dominant males may engage in mate guarding, where they closely follow and protect females during their receptive period. Mate guarding helps ensure the exclusive mating access of the guarding male and can reduce the chances of other males mating with the female.

6.1.8 Pregnancy and Birth
Gestation Period:

The gestation period in squirrel monkeys is approximately 150 to 170 days, depending on the species. After successful mating and conception, females undergo pregnancy.

Birth and Parental Care:

Female squirrel monkeys give birth to a single offspring, occasionally twins. Both males and females participate in parental care, with males engaging in grooming and protection of the infant. Cooperative care contributes to the survival and well-being of the offspring.

In summary, the mating behavior of squirrel monkeys is a complex and dynamic process influenced by social structures, reproductive cycles, courtship displays, and individual interactions. These behaviors contribute to the reproductive success of the species and play a crucial role in maintaining the social cohesion and dynamics within the troop.

6.2 Gestation and Birth

Gestation and birth are critical phases in the reproductive cycle of squirrel monkeys. These processes involve physiological changes in females, the development of the embryo or fetus, and the eventual birth of offspring. Understanding the details of gestation and birth in squirrel monkeys provides insights into their reproductive strategies, parental care, and the factors influencing the survival of their young.

6.2 Gestation and Birth in Squirrel Monkeys
6.2.1 Reproductive Physiology
Estrus and Mating:

Female squirrel monkeys experience estrus cycles, during which they become sexually receptive. Mating typically occurs during the female's estrus period, leading to the potential fertilization of eggs.

Ovulation and Fertilization:

Squirrel monkeys, like many primates, undergo spontaneous ovulation. Once ovulation occurs, fertilization can take place if the female mates with a male during this fertile period. Fertilization marks the beginning of gestation.

6.2.2 Gestation Period
Duration of Gestation:

The gestation period in squirrel monkeys varies depending on the species. On average, the gestation period is approximately 150 to 170 days. The length of gestation can be influenced by factors such as species-specific variations and individual health.

Physiological Changes:

During gestation, females undergo physiological changes to support the developing fetus. These changes include hormonal adjustments, increased blood flow to the uterus, and the development of structures like the placenta to facilitate nutrient exchange between the mother and the developing offspring.

6.2.3 Pregnancy and Parental Care

Cooperative Parental Care:

Both males and females in squirrel monkey troops engage in cooperative parental care. While the female carries the physiological burden of gestation, males contribute to the care of offspring. This cooperative care is vital for the well-being and survival of the young.

Grooming and Protection:

Males may engage in grooming behaviors towards pregnant females, providing a supportive social environment. After birth, both males and females participate in grooming the newborn, forming social bonds and contributing to the infant's physical well-being.

6.2.4 Birth Process

Single Births and Occasional Twins:

Squirrel monkeys typically give birth to a single offspring, although occasional twin births may occur. The birth of twins is less common and may present additional challenges for the female in terms of parental care.

Safe Birth Environment:

Females often seek a safe and secluded location for giving birth, such as a hidden spot in the vegetation or a protected tree hollow. This behavior helps protect the vulnerable newborn from potential predators.

Post-Birth Recovery:

After giving birth, females undergo a period of post-birth recovery. During this time, they may continue to receive support from the troop, including grooming and protection. The female's recovery is essential for her overall health and the successful care of the offspring.

6.2.5 Infant Development
Altricial Offspring:

Squirrel monkey infants are born in an altricial state, meaning they are relatively undeveloped and dependent on parental care. The newborns are typically small, with closed eyes and limited mobility.

Carrying on Mother's Back:

One distinctive aspect of squirrel monkey parental care is the carrying of infants on the mother's back. The mother provides protection and transportation for the infant, enhancing the infant's chances of survival during the early stages of development.

Weaning and Independence:

The weaning process in squirrel monkeys involves a transition from maternal milk to solid food. Weaning marks the beginning of increased independence for the offspring, although they continue to benefit from the protection and guidance of the troop.

6.2.6 Factors Influencing Reproductive Success
Environmental Conditions:

The availability of resources, climatic conditions, and the overall health of the ecosystem can influence the reproductive success of squirrel monkeys. Adequate food resources and a stable environment contribute to successful gestation, birth, and the survival of offspring. Social Support:

The social dynamics within the troop, including cooperative parental care and support from other group members, play a crucial role in reproductive success. Social support enhances the chances of survival for both the mother and her offspring.

Predation and Threats:

The risk of predation and exposure to threats can impact the reproductive success of squirrel monkeys. The choice of birthing sites and the ability to detect and respond to potential dangers are crucial for ensuring the safety of the mother and her young.

In conclusion, gestation and birth in squirrel monkeys involve a series of complex physiological processes, cooperative parental care, and adaptations to environmental conditions. The reproductive success of squirrel monkeys is influenced by various factors, highlighting the intricate interplay between biological, social, and ecological elements in their reproductive strategies.

6.3 Parental Care

Parental care in squirrel monkeys is a complex and cooperative process involving both males and females within the troop. This care encompasses various behaviors that contribute to the well-being, protection, and development of offspring. Understanding the dynamics of parental care sheds light on the social structure of squirrel monkey troops, the adaptive strategies for raising offspring in the tropical rainforest, and the roles of both parents in ensuring the survival of the young.

6.3 Parental Care in Squirrel Monkeys
6.3.1 Cooperative Parenting
Males' Involvement:

One distinctive feature of squirrel monkey parental care is the active involvement of both males and females. Males contribute significantly to the care of offspring, engaging in behaviors that support the mother and the young.

Grooming and Affiliation:

Parental care often involves grooming behaviors, where individuals within the troop engage in mutual grooming.

Grooming not only strengthens social bonds but also contributes to the cleanliness and health of the mother and her offspring.

6.3.2 Protection and Vigilance
Predator Deterrence:

Parental care includes protective measures to ensure the safety of the infant. Both parents and other troop members may actively engage in vigilance behaviors to detect and deter potential predators. This collective effort enhances the survival chances of the offspring.

Carrying and Sheltering:

Mothers often carry their infants on their backs, providing a secure and mobile shelter for the young. This carrying behavior not only offers protection from potential threats but also facilitates the mother's ability to forage and move through the forest canopy.

6.3.3 Communication and Social Bonds
Vocalizations and Signals:

Communication plays a vital role in parental care. Vocalizations, body language, and other signals are used to convey information within the troop. Mothers may use specific vocalizations to communicate with their infants, and group members share information to coordinate protective efforts.

Social Bonds and Cohesion:

Parental care strengthens social bonds within the troop. Grooming, affiliative behaviors, and shared responsibilities contribute to the overall cohesion of the group. Strong social bonds enhance cooperation and support, fostering a stable environment for raising offspring.

6.3.4 Nutritional Support
Lactation and Nursing:

Maternal care involves the provision of nourishment through lactation. Female squirrel monkeys nurse their infants, providing them with essential nutrients for growth and development. Lactation is a crucial aspect of maternal care that contributes to the overall health of the offspring.

Transition to Solid Food:

As the infant grows, there is a transition from exclusive reliance on maternal milk to the incorporation of solid food. This weaning process is gradual, and offspring may continue to receive support and guidance from the mother and other troop members as they explore and learn to forage independently.

6.3.5 Learning and Socialization
Observational Learning:

Parental care involves opportunities for observational learning. Young squirrel monkeys learn essential skills by observing the behaviors of their parents and other troop members. This learning process contributes to the acquisition of foraging techniques, social behaviors, and adaptive strategies.

Socialization within the Troop:

Parental care extends beyond the nuclear family unit to include socialization within the entire troop. Offspring interact with other troop members, developing social skills, and establishing relationships that contribute to their integration into the group.

6.3.6 Long-Term Involvement
Extended Care by Males:

The involvement of males in parental care extends beyond infancy. In some cases, males continue to play a role in caring for offspring even after weaning. This extended care reinforces social bonds and may contribute to the overall success and resilience of the troop.

Reproductive Success and Troop Dynamics:

The success of parental care contributes to reproductive success within the troop. Offspring that receive adequate care, protection, and support are more likely to reach reproductive age, contributing to the continuation of the species and the stability of the troop dynamics.

6.3.7 Adaptations to Environmental Challenges
Flexible Parenting Strategies:

Squirrel monkeys exhibit flexibility in their parenting strategies. The ability to adapt to environmental challenges, such as changes in resource availability or the presence of predators, is crucial for the survival of offspring.

Cooperation in Resource Acquisition:

Parental care is intertwined with cooperative behaviors related to resource acquisition. Cooperative foraging, communication about food sources, and sharing of resources contribute to the overall success of the troop in providing for the needs of both parents and offspring.
In summary, parental care in squirrel monkeys is a multifaceted and cooperative process that involves both males and females within the troop. The collective effort in protection, grooming, communication, and nutritional support contributes to the successful raising of offspring in the dynamic and challenging environment of the tropical rainforest. The intricate social structure and behaviors associated with parental care reflect the adaptability and resilience of squirrel monkeys as they navigate the complexities of their natural habitat.

CHAPTER SEVEN

Predators and Threats

7.1 Natural Predators

Squirrel monkeys, like many other species, face threats from various natural predators in their native habitats. These predators play a crucial role in shaping the ecology of the tropical rainforests where squirrel monkeys reside. Understanding the natural predators of squirrel monkeys provides insights into the dynamics of predator-prey interactions and the adaptations that squirrel monkeys have developed to survive in their complex ecosystems.

7.1.1 Birds of Prey
Harpy Eagles (Harpia harpyja):

Harpy eagles are formidable raptors found in the rainforests of Central and South America. With powerful talons and keen eyesight, harpy eagles are capable hunters and pose a significant threat to squirrel monkeys. They may ambush and capture monkeys as they move through the canopy.

Crested Eagles (Morphnus guianensis):

Crested eagles are another avian predator known to inhabit the same regions as squirrel monkeys. These eagles are adept at navigating through the forest canopy and may target arboreal prey, including squirrel monkeys, as part of their diet.

7.1.2 Large Snakes
Boa Constrictors (Boa constrictor):

Boa constrictors are constricting snakes found in tropical regions, including the habitats of squirrel monkeys. These snakes are capable of climbing trees and may ambush primates, including squirrel monkeys, as they traverse the branches. Boa constrictors use constriction to subdue and consume their prey.
Tree Pythons (Morelia viridis):

Tree pythons are arboreal constrictors that may pose a threat to squirrel monkeys. These snakes are well-adapted to life in the trees and may actively hunt for small primates, including squirrel monkeys, by ambushing them in the dense vegetation.

7.1.3 Felids (Cats)

Ocelots (Leopardus pardalis):

Ocelots are medium-sized wild cats found in the rainforests of Central and South America. These agile and nocturnal predators are capable of climbing trees and may hunt squirrel monkeys. Ocelots are known for their adaptability and diverse diet, which includes various small mammals.

Margay Cats (Leopardus wiedii):

Margay cats are arboreal felids closely related to ocelots. With excellent climbing abilities, margays are well-suited to hunting in the forest canopy. They may prey on squirrel monkeys and other small mammals by ambushing them from above.

7.1.4 Raptors

Hawks and Accipiters:

Various species of hawks and accipiters are known to prey on small mammals, including squirrel monkeys. These birds of prey use their sharp talons and beaks to capture and consume agile targets within the forest canopy.

7.1.5 Arboreal Mammals
Tayras (Eira barbara):

Tayras, also known as bush dogs, are arboreal members of the weasel family found in Central and South American rainforests. They are agile climbers and may hunt in the canopy, posing a potential threat to squirrel monkeys.

7.1.6 Monitor Lizards
Green Iguanas (Iguana iguana):

While primarily herbivorous, green iguanas may opportunistically prey on smaller animals, including young or juvenile squirrel monkeys. Their climbing abilities allow them to access arboreal habitats where squirrel monkeys may be vulnerable.

7.1.7 Domestic and Feral Animals
Domestic Cats and Dogs:

In areas where human settlements encroach upon natural habitats, domestic cats and dogs may pose a threat to squirrel monkeys. Both domestic and feral animals may hunt squirrel monkeys, leading to increased predation risk in fragmented habitats.

7.1.8 Behavioral Adaptations
Vigilance and Alarm Calls:

Squirrel monkeys exhibit vigilant behaviors and employ alarm calls to alert group members of potential threats. These vocalizations help mobilize the troop to adopt defensive measures against predators.

Group Living:

Living in social groups, or troops, provides squirrel monkeys with collective protection against predators. The increased number of vigilant individuals enhances the chances of detecting predators early, and group members may collaborate to repel or escape from potential threats.

Arboreal Adaptations:

The arboreal lifestyle of squirrel monkeys, with their agility in navigating the forest canopy, serves as a defensive adaptation. By spending the majority of their time in trees, they reduce their vulnerability to ground-dwelling predators.

Cryptic Coloration:

Squirrel monkeys often exhibit cryptic coloration, with fur patterns that blend with the surrounding foliage. This adaptation helps them avoid detection by visually-oriented predators, providing a degree of camouflage.

In conclusion, squirrel monkeys face a range of natural predators in their tropical rainforest habitats. These predators include birds of prey, large snakes, felids, raptors, arboreal mammals, and, in some cases, domestic animals. Squirrel monkeys have developed behavioral and physical adaptations to mitigate predation risk, relying on group living, vigilance, alarm calls, and their arboreal lifestyle to enhance their chances of survival in the complex and dynamic ecosystems they inhabit.

7.2 Human-Induced Threats

Squirrel monkeys, like many other wildlife species, face various human-induced threats that pose significant challenges to their survival and well-being. These threats are often associated with human activities that directly or indirectly impact the natural habitats and ecosystems where squirrel monkeys reside. Understanding these human-induced threats is crucial for developing conservation strategies aimed at preserving these primates and their environments.

7.2 Human-Induced Threats to Squirrel Monkeys
7.2.1 Habitat Loss and Fragmentation
Deforestation:

One of the most significant threats to squirrel monkeys is habitat loss due to deforestation. The expansion of agriculture, logging, and infrastructure development leads to the clearing of large areas of tropical rainforests, reducing the available habitat for squirrel monkeys.

Habitat Fragmentation:

Habitat fragmentation results from the subdivision of continuous forest into smaller, isolated patches. This process disrupts the natural connectivity of ecosystems and can lead to increased isolation of squirrel monkey populations. Fragmentation makes it more challenging for individuals to find mates, food, and suitable territories.

7.2.2 Logging and Timber Harvesting
Commercial Logging:

Logging activities, including the extraction of timber for commercial purposes, can directly impact squirrel monkey habitats. The removal of trees reduces the availability of suitable nesting sites, disrupts foraging routes, and alters the overall structure of the forest ecosystem.

Selective Logging:

Even selective logging practices, where specific tree species are targeted, can have cascading effects on the ecology of the forest. Changes in vegetation composition and structure can affect the availability of food resources for squirrel monkeys and impact the diversity of plant species that they rely on.

7.2.3 Agricultural Expansion

Crop Cultivation:

The expansion of agricultural activities, including the cultivation of crops such as palm oil, soy, and other commodities, contributes to the conversion of natural habitats into farmland. This process directly removes important foraging areas and further reduces the available space for squirrel monkeys.

Agrochemicals:

The use of agrochemicals, such as pesticides and fertilizers, in agricultural areas can have detrimental effects on the health of squirrel monkeys. Exposure to these chemicals may lead to direct poisoning or impact the quality of food resources, affecting the overall fitness of the population.

7.2.4 Infrastructure Development

Road Construction:

Infrastructure development, particularly the construction of roads, can have negative consequences for squirrel monkeys. Roads can act as barriers, limiting the movement of individuals and increasing the risk of road mortality. Additionally, roads may facilitate access for illegal activities such as hunting and logging.

Urbanization:

Urban expansion encroaches upon natural habitats, leading to the conversion of forested areas into urban landscapes. Urbanization brings with it pollution, habitat destruction, and increased human-wildlife conflicts, all of which negatively impact squirrel monkey populations.

7.2.5 Hunting and Poaching

Bushmeat Trade:

Squirrel monkeys are often hunted for the bushmeat trade, where their meat is consumed by local communities. The demand for bushmeat poses a direct threat to squirrel monkey populations, especially in regions where hunting is unsustainable.

Pet Trade:

The pet trade is another threat to squirrel monkeys, as they are sometimes captured and sold as exotic pets. This not only reduces wild populations but also subjects individual animals to stress, captivity-related health issues, and inappropriate living conditions.

7.2.6 Climate Change
Altered Climate Patterns:

Climate change can have indirect effects on squirrel monkeys by altering the distribution of plant and insect species that make up their diet. Changes in temperature, precipitation patterns, and extreme weather events can impact the availability of food resources and disrupt the balance of ecosystems.

Habitat Shifts:

The shifting climate may also lead to changes in the distribution of suitable habitats for squirrel monkeys. As climatic conditions alter, the composition and structure of forests may shift, affecting the overall suitability of these areas for primate species.

7.2.7 Disease Transmission
Zoonotic Diseases:

Human activities and interactions, including habitat disturbance and encroachment, can increase the risk of disease transmission between humans and wildlife. Squirrel monkeys may be susceptible to zoonotic diseases, which can have severe consequences for their health and population dynamics.

7.2.8 Conservation Challenges and Solutions
Conservation Efforts:

Conservation initiatives play a vital role in addressing human-induced threats to squirrel monkeys. Protected areas, wildlife corridors, and habitat restoration projects aim to mitigate the impacts of habitat loss and fragmentation.

Community Engagement:

Involving local communities in conservation efforts is essential. Community-based conservation approaches, sustainable resource management, and education programs can help build awareness and support for the protection of squirrel monkeys and their habitats.

Legislation and Enforcement:

Strengthening and enforcing laws against illegal hunting, logging, and wildlife trade are critical components of conservation efforts. Legal measures help curb activities that directly threaten squirrel monkeys and other wildlife species.

Research and Monitoring:

Continued research on the ecology, behavior, and health of squirrel monkeys is crucial for understanding their vulnerabilities and developing effective conservation strategies. Monitoring populations and tracking changes in their habitats provide valuable data for informed decision-making.

In summary, human-induced threats pose significant challenges to the survival of squirrel monkeys. The combination of habitat loss, hunting, climate change, and other factors requires comprehensive and collaborative conservation efforts to safeguard these primates and the biodiversity of their tropical rainforest ecosystems. Addressing these threats involves a combination of protective measures, sustainable resource management, community engagement, and the promotion of responsible development practices.

7.3 Conservation Status

The conservation status of a species is an assessment of its risk of extinction based on various factors, including population size, trends, and threats to its habitat and well-being. The International Union for Conservation of Nature (IUCN) provides a widely recognized and widely used system for classifying species into different categories based on their conservation status. These categories range from "Least Concern" to "Extinct," with intermediate categories such as "Near Threatened," "Vulnerable," "Endangered," and "Critically Endangered." The conservation status of squirrel monkeys is dependent on the specific species and regional populations.

7.3 Conservation Status of Squirrel Monkeys
7.3.1 Species-Specific Considerations
Variety of Species:

There are several species of squirrel monkeys, each with its own distribution range, habitat preferences, and ecological requirements. Conservation assessments need to be conducted on a species-specific basis to account for the unique characteristics of each.

7.3.2 Regional Populations

Habitat Fragmentation:
Some populations of squirrel monkeys may face higher conservation risks due to habitat fragmentation, which can lead to isolation, reduced genetic diversity, and increased vulnerability to environmental changes.

Local Threats:

Conservation status can vary between regional populations based on localized threats such as hunting, logging, and agricultural expansion. Understanding the specific challenges faced by each population is crucial for targeted conservation efforts.

7.3.3 Common Threats
Habitat Loss:

Habitat loss due to deforestation and land-use change is a primary threat to many squirrel monkey populations. As their natural habitats are cleared for agriculture, logging, or urban development, squirrel monkeys lose crucial resources and face increased vulnerability.
Hunting and Wildlife Trade:

Hunting for bushmeat and the wildlife trade pose direct threats to squirrel monkeys. The demand for their meat and their capture for the pet trade can have significant impacts on population numbers and dynamics.

Climate Change:

Climate change can affect the distribution of suitable habitats and impact the availability of food resources for squirrel monkeys. Changes in climate patterns may exacerbate existing threats and create new challenges for their survival.

7.3.4 Conservation Efforts

Protected Areas:

Establishing and maintaining protected areas, such as national parks and reserves, is a crucial conservation strategy. These areas provide safe havens for squirrel monkeys and other wildlife, allowing them to thrive without direct exposure to some human-induced threats.

Habitat Restoration:

Habitat restoration initiatives aim to rehabilitate degraded areas and reconnect fragmented habitats. Restoring natural habitats enhances the availability of resources and promotes the overall health and resilience of squirrel monkey populations.

Community-Based Conservation:

Engaging local communities in conservation efforts is essential. Community-based conservation initiatives involve collaborating with residents to promote sustainable practices, reduce hunting, and create a sense of shared responsibility for wildlife and their habitats.

Research and Monitoring:

Continued research on the ecology, behavior, and health of squirrel monkeys provides critical data for conservation planning. Monitoring population trends, habitat conditions, and the impacts of threats allows conservationists to adapt strategies based on up-to-date information.

7.3.5 IUCN Red List Status

Variable Status:

The IUCN Red List provides a standardized system for assessing the conservation status of species. Different species of squirrel monkeys may have varying Red List statuses based on their specific circumstances. As of my last knowledge update in January 2022, the specific Red List statuses for each species should be consulted for the most current information.

Examples of IUCN Status:

As of the last update, the Central American Squirrel Monkey (Saimiri oerstedii) was listed as "Least Concern," while the Black-Capped Squirrel Monkey (Saimiri boliviensis) had a status of "Vulnerable." It's crucial to consult the latest IUCN Red List assessments for the most current information on the conservation status of each species.

In conclusion, the conservation status of squirrel monkeys is influenced by a variety of factors, including habitat loss, hunting, climate change, and regional variations. Effective conservation requires species-specific assessments, targeted strategies addressing local threats, and collaborative efforts involving governments, communities, and conservation organizations. Regular monitoring and updating of conservation status assessments help ensure that management strategies remain relevant and adaptive to changing conditions.

CHAPTER EIGHT

Interaction with Humans

8.1 Squirrel Monkeys in Captivity

Squirrel monkeys are among the New World monkeys that are commonly kept in captivity, both in zoos and research facilities. These small primates are known for their active and social behavior, making them interesting subjects for observation and research. However, keeping squirrel monkeys in captivity also raises ethical and welfare concerns, and there are specific considerations regarding their care, environment, and well-being.

8.1.1 Ethical Considerations
Animal Welfare:

The welfare of squirrel monkeys in captivity is a primary ethical concern. Ensuring that their physical and psychological needs are met is crucial for promoting their well-being. This includes providing appropriate enclosures, social structures, and environmental enrichment.

Social Structure:

Squirrel monkeys are highly social animals that live in troops in the wild. Captive settings should aim to replicate natural social structures as much as possible, ensuring that individuals have opportunities for social interaction and the formation of social bonds.

8.1.2 Enclosures and Habitats
Space Requirements:

Squirrel monkeys require sufficient space to engage in natural behaviors such as climbing, jumping, and socializing. Enclosures should be designed to accommodate their arboreal nature, with elevated structures and ample opportunities for movement.

Environmental Enrichment:

Captive environments should be enriched to provide mental stimulation and opportunities for physical activity. This can include the provision of climbing structures, foraging opportunities, and objects that encourage exploration and play.

Naturalistic Features:

Mimicking natural elements of their habitat, such as trees, branches, and vegetation, contributes to the well-being of captive squirrel monkeys. Providing hiding spots, platforms, and varied textures enhances the complexity of their environment.

8.1.3 Social Dynamics

Group Living:

Squirrel monkeys are social animals that thrive in group settings. Whenever possible, individuals should be housed in social groups to allow for natural interactions and social hierarchies. Group living also provides social support and can reduce stress.

Introduction Protocols:

Introducing new individuals to an established group requires careful planning and monitoring. Protocols should be in place to ensure a smooth integration process, reducing the risk of aggression and stress among group members.

8.1.4 Nutrition and Diet

Varied Diet:

Captive squirrel monkeys should receive a nutritionally balanced and varied diet that mimics their natural foraging behavior. This includes a mix of fruits, vegetables, leaves, and appropriate protein sources. Diets should be formulated to meet their specific nutritional requirements.

Foraging Opportunities:

Providing opportunities for foraging and food-related activities helps stimulate natural behaviors. This can involve hiding food items in the enclosure, using puzzle feeders, or presenting food in ways that encourage exploration.

8.1.5 Veterinary Care
Health Monitoring:

Regular health check-ups and monitoring are essential for captive squirrel monkeys. Veterinarians with expertise in primate care should be involved in their healthcare, addressing both preventive measures and the management of any medical conditions.

Behavioral Observation:

Monitoring behavioral patterns is crucial for detecting signs of stress, illness, or abnormal behavior. Observations by caretakers and researchers can provide insights into the overall well-being of the animals.

8.1.6 Research and Educational Programs
Behavioral Studies:

Squirrel monkeys in captivity can contribute to scientific research, particularly in the fields of behavior, cognition, and psychology. Ethical research practices should prioritize the well-being of the animals and adhere to established guidelines.

Educational Outreach:

Captive squirrel monkeys in zoos and educational facilities can serve as ambassadors for their wild counterparts. Educational programs can raise awareness about the species, their natural behaviors, and the importance of conservation efforts.

8.1.7 Conservation Role

Species Survival Programs:
Captive breeding programs, often part of Species Survival Programs (SSPs) in zoos, aim to maintain genetically diverse populations of squirrel monkeys. These programs can serve as a safety net for the species and contribute to overall conservation efforts.

Reintroduction Considerations:

In some cases, captive-bred squirrel monkeys may be considered for reintroduction into their natural habitats. Such programs require careful planning, considering factors such as genetic diversity, health status, and the availability of suitable release sites.

8.1.8 Legal and Ethical Regulations
Animal Welfare Laws:

Captivity conditions for squirrel monkeys are often subject to local and international animal welfare laws and regulations. These guidelines are in place to ensure ethical treatment, proper care, and humane conditions for captive animals.

Accreditation and Certification:

Zoological institutions often seek accreditation from relevant authorities or organizations that set standards for animal care and welfare. Certification ensures that institutions adhere to established guidelines and practices.

In conclusion, the captivity of squirrel monkeys involves a complex balance between the interests of scientific research, educational outreach, and the ethical treatment of individual animals. Maintaining high standards of care, prioritizing the well-being of the monkeys, and contributing to conservation efforts are key considerations for institutions and organizations involved in the captive management of squirrel monkeys. Regular evaluation, adherence to ethical guidelines, and ongoing research contribute to the continuous improvement of practices related to the care of squirrel monkeys in captivity.

8.2 Research Importance

Research on squirrel monkeys holds significant importance for several reasons, encompassing both scientific understanding and broader conservation efforts. These primates, known for their social behavior, complex cognition, and arboreal lifestyles, serve as valuable subjects in various fields of study. Understanding the importance of research on squirrel monkeys involves considerations related to behavioral ecology, comparative cognition, biomedical research, conservation, and education.

8.2 Importance of Research on Squirrel Monkeys
8.2.1 Behavioral Ecology

Social Dynamics:

Research on squirrel monkeys contributes to our understanding of their social organization, group dynamics, and communication. Studying their social structures, hierarchies, and affiliative behaviors provides insights into the evolution of sociality in primates.

Foraging and Feeding Behavior:

Investigating how squirrel monkeys forage for food, select resources, and utilize their environments enhances our understanding of their ecological role.

Such studies contribute to broader ecological research on tropical rainforest ecosystems.

Habitat Use and Niche Specialization:

Research on habitat use and niche specialization helps elucidate how squirrel monkeys adapt to their environments. Understanding their preferences for certain tree species, canopy heights, and ecological niches informs conservation strategies and habitat management.

8.2.2 Comparative Cognition

Cognitive Abilities:

Squirrel monkeys exhibit advanced cognitive abilities, making them valuable subjects for comparative cognition studies. Research on their problem-solving skills, memory, and learning abilities contributes to our understanding of primate cognition and evolution.

Communication Studies:

Investigating the vocalizations, facial expressions, and gestural communication of squirrel monkeys helps unravel the complexities of primate communication.

Comparative studies shed light on the evolution of communication systems in primates, including humans.

8.2.3 Biomedical Research

Disease Research and Modeling:

Squirrel monkeys have been used in biomedical research, including studies on infectious diseases and vaccine development. Their physiological and immunological similarities to humans make them valuable models for understanding disease processes and testing medical interventions.

Neuroscience and Brain Research:

Due to their close genetic and physiological resemblance to humans, squirrel monkeys are used in neuroscience research. Studies on their brains and neural systems provide insights into brain function, development, and disorders, with potential implications for human health.

8.2.4 Conservation

Population Dynamics:

Research on the population dynamics of squirrel monkeys in the wild helps assess their status, monitor population trends, and identify factors affecting their survival. This information is critical for conservation planning and the development of effective management strategies.

Habitat Conservation:

Understanding the habitat requirements, ranging patterns, and resource needs of squirrel monkeys informs habitat conservation efforts. Research contributes to the identification and protection of key habitats, corridors, and biodiversity hotspots.

Conservation Genetics:

Genetic studies provide information on the genetic diversity, gene flow, and relatedness of squirrel monkey populations. Conservation genetic research helps design strategies to maintain genetic variability and mitigate the risks associated with small and isolated populations.

8.2.5 Education and Outreach
Public Awareness:

Research findings contribute to public awareness and education about squirrel monkeys. Zoos, wildlife sanctuaries, and educational institutions can use research-based information to engage the public in conservation initiatives and promote an appreciation for biodiversity.

Curriculum Development:

Research on squirrel monkeys can be integrated into educational curricula, enhancing science education at various levels. By incorporating real-world examples, educators can inspire students to pursue careers in science, biology, and conservation.

8.2.6 Ethical and Welfare Considerations
Improving Captive Care:

Research on squirrel monkeys in captivity contributes to the improvement of their welfare by identifying optimal housing conditions, dietary requirements, and enrichment strategies. Ethical research practices prioritize the well-being of captive individuals.

Behavioral Management:

Understanding the natural behaviors of squirrel monkeys helps develop behavioral management protocols in captivity. Providing opportunities for species-typical behaviors, social interactions, and mental stimulation is essential for their overall well-being.

In conclusion, research on squirrel monkeys plays a crucial role in expanding our knowledge of primate biology, behavior, cognition, and ecology. The insights gained from such research have implications for wildlife conservation, habitat management, biomedical advancements, and education. Ethical research practices ensure that the welfare of squirrel monkeys, both in the wild and in captivity, is prioritized, contributing to a holistic approach to primate research and conservation.

8.3 Ecotourism and Conservation Education

Ecotourism and conservation education play vital roles in promoting awareness, understanding, and support for wildlife conservation, including species like squirrel monkeys. These approaches leverage tourism and educational initiatives to foster a connection between people and the natural world, encouraging sustainable practices, habitat protection, and species preservation.

8.3 Ecotourism and Conservation Education
8.3.1 Ecotourism
Definition:

Ecotourism refers to responsible travel to natural areas that conserves the environment, sustains the well-being of local communities, and educates visitors. In the context of squirrel monkeys, ecotourism can provide opportunities for people to observe and appreciate these primates in their natural habitats.

Benefits:

Economic Support: Ecotourism can generate revenue for local communities and conservation initiatives. Entrance fees, guided tours, and related services contribute to the financial sustainability of protected areas and conservation projects.

Local Empowerment: When well-managed, ecotourism can empower local communities by creating jobs, supporting small businesses, and fostering community engagement in conservation efforts. This can lead to a sense of shared responsibility for protecting natural resources.

Conservation Funding: Revenues generated from ecotourism activities can be reinvested into habitat conservation, anti-poaching efforts, and wildlife research. This direct financial support enhances the capacity for conservation initiatives.

Challenges:

Disturbance to Wildlife: Improperly managed ecotourism can lead to disturbances to wildlife, including squirrel monkeys. Excessive noise, close proximity to animals, and alterations to natural behaviors can have negative impacts on the well-being of the primates.

Habitat Degradation: If not carefully regulated, increased human activity associated with ecotourism can lead to habitat degradation. Trails, infrastructure, and waste management associated with tourism can have unintended consequences on natural ecosystems.

8.3.2 Conservation Education

Definition:

Conservation education involves raising awareness, imparting knowledge, and fostering positive attitudes towards conservation. It aims to inspire individuals to make informed decisions that contribute to the protection of the environment and wildlife.

Components:

Environmental Awareness: Conservation education aims to increase awareness about the importance of biodiversity, ecosystems, and the interconnectedness of all living organisms. Understanding the role of species like squirrel monkeys in their ecosystems is a key component.

Scientific Literacy: Providing scientific knowledge about the biology, behavior, and ecological roles of squirrel monkeys enhances public understanding. Knowledgeable individuals are more likely to appreciate the importance of conservation.

Behavioral Change: Conservation education seeks to influence behavior by promoting sustainable practices, responsible tourism, and ethical choices that contribute to the well-being of wildlife and their habitats.

Outreach Methods:

School Programs: Educational programs in schools and universities can incorporate lessons about wildlife conservation, ecology, and the importance of preserving natural habitats. Field trips and hands-on activities enhance learning experiences.

Public Events: Workshops, seminars, and public events focused on conservation topics provide platforms for experts to share knowledge and engage with the public. Zoos, botanical gardens, and nature reserves often organize such events.

Digital Media and Technology: The use of digital media, including websites, documentaries, social media, and mobile applications, facilitates wide-reaching conservation education. Virtual experiences and online resources can educate a global audience.

8.3.3 Synergy Between Ecotourism and Conservation Education

Visitor Interpretation Centers:

Ecotourism destinations can incorporate visitor interpretation centers that provide educational resources, interactive displays, and guided information sessions. These centers serve as hubs for conservation education, ensuring that visitors leave with a deeper understanding of the natural environment and the species they encounter.

Guided Tours with Educational Components:

Well-designed ecotourism experiences include guided tours led by knowledgeable naturalists or guides. These guides can provide educational insights into the behavior, ecology, and conservation status of squirrel monkeys, fostering a sense of appreciation and responsibility among visitors.

Community Involvement and Education:

Integrating local communities into ecotourism initiatives and conservation education efforts is essential. Community members can contribute valuable cultural insights, and their involvement enhances the authenticity and effectiveness of educational programs.

Promotion of Responsible Tourism Practices:

Conservation education in the context of ecotourism emphasizes responsible and ethical behavior. This includes guidelines for wildlife observation, minimizing environmental impact, and supporting local conservation initiatives. Informed and responsible tourists are more likely to contribute positively to conservation.

8.3.4 Measuring Impact and Success
Visitor Surveys and Feedback:

Gathering feedback from ecotourism participants and conservation education program attendees helps measure the impact of these initiatives. Understanding the level of knowledge gained, attitudes changed, and behaviors influenced provides valuable insights.

Long-Term Monitoring:

The success of ecotourism and conservation education efforts can be assessed through long-term monitoring of biodiversity, habitat health, and community engagement. Positive trends in these indicators may indicate the effectiveness of conservation initiatives.

Collaboration with Research Institutions:

Collaboration with research institutions allows for the integration of scientific research into ecotourism and education programs. Monitoring wildlife populations, studying habitat dynamics, and assessing the socio-economic impacts of ecotourism contribute to evidence-based conservation practices.

In conclusion, ecotourism and conservation education are powerful tools for raising awareness, generating support, and fostering responsible behavior towards wildlife and their habitats. When implemented thoughtfully and with a focus on sustainability, these initiatives can contribute to the conservation of species like squirrel monkeys, ensuring that they thrive in their natural environments while providing benefits to local communities.

CHAPTER NINE

9.1 Common Squirrel Monkey (Saimiri sciureus)
The Common Squirrel Monkey (Saimiri sciureus), also known simply as the Squirrel Monkey, is a species of New World monkey that belongs to the family Cebidae. They are small, agile primates known for their distinctive appearance, social behavior, and lively antics. Native to the tropical rainforests of South America, Common Squirrel Monkeys are highly adapted to arboreal life and are characterized by their large eyes, bushy tails, and contrasting fur patterns.

9.1.1 Physical Characteristics
Size:

Common Squirrel Monkeys are relatively small primates, with an average length ranging from 10 to 14 inches (25 to 35 cm). Their tails are often longer than their bodies, measuring around 14 to 18 inches (35 to 45 cm).
Fur Coloration:

They have a distinctive fur pattern with a mix of colors. The fur on their bodies is typically olive or grayish-green, while their limbs and the lower part of their faces are yellow or orange. Their backs are marked with a white or yellowish stripe, and their underparts are lighter in color.

Facial Features:

Common Squirrel Monkeys have large, round eyes that face forward, providing them with good depth perception. Their noses are small and flat, and they have a bare face with dark skin around their eyes.

Tail:

One of their notable features is their long, bushy tail, which is not prehensile. The tail is often used for balance while moving through the trees, and it is not capable of grasping objects.

9.1.2 Distribution and Habitat
Native Range:

The Common Squirrel Monkey is found in the tropical rainforests of South America. Their range includes parts of Brazil, Colombia, Ecuador, Peru, and Venezuela.
Habitat:

They primarily inhabit the canopy of the rainforest and are well-adapted to an arboreal lifestyle. Squirrel monkeys are highly agile and can move quickly through the treetops.

9.1.3 Behavior and Social Structure
Diurnal and Arboreal:

Common Squirrel Monkeys are diurnal, meaning they are active during the day. They spend the majority of their time in the trees, using their strong hind limbs and prehensile tails to move through the branches.

Social Structure:

These monkeys are highly social and live in multi-male, multi-female groups known as troops. Troops can consist of up to 300 individuals, though average group sizes are smaller. Within the troop, there is a social

hierarchy, and grooming is an important aspect of social bonding.
Communication:

Squirrel monkeys communicate using various vocalizations, including chirps, whistles, and chattering sounds. They also use facial expressions and body language to convey information within the group.

9.1.4 Diet and Foraging
Omnivorous Diet:

Common Squirrel Monkeys are omnivores, feeding on a varied diet that includes fruits, insects, leaves, flowers, and small vertebrates. They are known to be opportunistic feeders, adjusting their diet based on seasonal availability.

Foraging Behavior:

Their foraging behavior involves searching for food in the canopy, using their agile movements to reach different parts of the trees. They may leap from branch to branch and even use their tails for balance while reaching for distant food sources.

9.1.5 Reproduction and Life Cycle

Breeding Season:

Breeding in squirrel monkeys typically occurs during the wet season when food resources are more abundant.

Gestation and Birth:

The gestation period is around 150 to 170 days, after which females give birth to a single offspring. The newborn clings to the mother's fur and is cared for by both parents and other members of the troop.

Maturation and Lifespan:

Squirrel monkeys reach sexual maturity at around 2 to 2.5 years of age. Their lifespan in the wild is approximately 15 years, although this can vary based on factors such as predation and environmental conditions.

9.1.6 Predators and Threats

Natural Predators:

Common Squirrel Monkeys face threats from various natural predators, including birds of prey, large snakes, and felids such as ocelots and margays.

Habitat Threats:

Habitat loss due to deforestation, logging, and agricultural activities poses a significant threat to squirrel monkeys. Fragmentation of their natural habitat can lead to isolation and increased vulnerability.

9.1.7 Conservation Status
IUCN Red List:
Conservation Measures:

Conservation efforts focus on protecting their natural habitats, implementing sustainable forestry practices, and raising awareness about the importance of preserving biodiversity.

In summary, the Common Squirrel Monkey is a captivating primate species known for its vibrant fur patterns, social behavior, and arboreal lifestyle. While they face threats from habitat loss and natural predators, conservation efforts aim to ensure the continued survival of this species in the diverse ecosystems of South American rainforests.

9.2 Other Squirrel Monkey Species

Aside from the Common Squirrel Monkey (Saimiri sciureus), there are several other species within the Saimiri genus, commonly known as squirrel monkeys. Each species has its own unique characteristics, distribution, and ecological adaptations. Below, I'll provide information on a few other notable squirrel monkey species:

9.2 Other Squirrel Monkey Species

9.2.1 Black-Capped Squirrel Monkey (Saimiri boliviensis)

Distribution:

The Black-Capped Squirrel Monkey, also known as the Bolivian Squirrel Monkey, is found in the rainforests of Bolivia, Brazil, and Peru.

Physical Characteristics:

It is characterized by a black cap on its head, contrasting with its yellowish-orange fur. The rest of its body has a similar coloration to the Common Squirrel Monkey.

Social Structure:

Like the Common Squirrel Monkey, the Black-Capped Squirrel Monkey lives in social groups, typically consisting of multiple males and females.

Conservation Status:

The Black-Capped Squirrel Monkey is classified as "Vulnerable" on the IUCN Red List due to habitat loss and fragmentation.

9.2.2 Central American Squirrel Monkey (Saimiri oerstedii)
Distribution:

The Central American Squirrel Monkey is found in the rainforests of Central America, including parts of Costa Rica and Panama.

Physical Characteristics:

It has a similar appearance to the Common Squirrel Monkey, with a mixture of olive, yellow, and orange fur. However, the Central American species may have a more limited distribution range.

Habitat and Behavior:

This species primarily inhabits lowland rainforests and exhibits similar behaviors to other squirrel monkeys, including an arboreal lifestyle and social group living.

Conservation Status:

The conservation status of the Central American Squirrel Monkey varies across its range, with some populations facing threats due to habitat loss and fragmentation.

9.2.3 Colombian Squirrel Monkey (Saimiri cassiquiarensis)
Distribution:

The Colombian Squirrel Monkey is found in parts of Colombia, Venezuela, and Brazil.

Physical Characteristics:

It has a distinctive color pattern with a black cap on its head, contrasting with its light-colored face. The fur on its back is typically grayish-brown, and its underparts are lighter.

Social Structure:

Like other squirrel monkeys, the Colombian species lives in social groups, and its behavior is characterized by cooperation and grooming.

Conservation Status:

The conservation status of the Colombian Squirrel Monkey varies across its range. Some populations may face threats due to habitat degradation and hunting.

9.2.4 Yellow Squirrel Monkey (Saimiri vanzolinii)
Distribution:

The Yellow Squirrel Monkey is found in Brazil, specifically in the Amazon rainforest.

Physical Characteristics:

This species has a bright yellow or golden coloration, making it distinct from other squirrel monkey species. Its face is dark, and it lacks the black cap seen in some other species.

Behavior and Ecology:

The Yellow Squirrel Monkey exhibits similar arboreal and social behaviors, including living in groups and foraging for a variety of foods.

Conservation Status:

The Yellow Squirrel Monkey faces threats from habitat loss and hunting, and its conservation status may be vulnerable in certain regions.

Conservation Considerations for Squirrel Monkey Species:
Habitat Preservation: Protecting and preserving the natural habitats of squirrel monkeys is crucial for their survival. This involves efforts to combat deforestation, establish protected areas, and promote sustainable land-use practices.

Anti-Poaching Measures: Implementing measures to prevent illegal hunting and the wildlife trade is essential for the conservation of squirrel monkey species. This includes enforcing laws and regulations, as well as raising awareness about the impacts of hunting.

Research and Monitoring: Continued research on the behavior, ecology, and population dynamics of different squirrel monkey species provides valuable information for conservation strategies. Regular monitoring helps assess the health of populations and the effectiveness of conservation initiatives.

Community Engagement: Involving local communities in conservation efforts fosters a sense of shared responsibility and can lead to more sustainable practices. Collaborative approaches that consider the needs and perspectives of local residents are vital.

Education and Awareness: Public awareness campaigns and educational programs play a crucial role in garnering support for squirrel monkey conservation. These initiatives inform communities, policymakers, and the general public about the importance of protecting these primates and their habitats.

In summary, the various squirrel monkey species face common threats such as habitat loss and fragmentation, as well as specific challenges unique to their geographic ranges. Conservation efforts must be tailored to the specific needs of each species, considering factors such as distribution, behavior, and the socio-economic context of the regions where they are found. Collaborative and multidisciplinary approaches are essential for the successful conservation of squirrel monkeys and the preservation of their natural habitats.

CHAPTER TEN

Fun Facts and Trivia

10.1 Unique Adaptations

Squirrel monkeys, like many other primate species, have evolved a set of unique adaptations that enable them to thrive in their specific ecological niche. These adaptations are a result of natural selection over generations and are finely tuned to their arboreal and social lifestyle in the tropical rainforests of South and Central America. Below are several unique adaptations that distinguish squirrel monkeys:

10.1 Unique Adaptations of Squirrel Monkeys
10.1.1 Arboreal Adaptations
1. Prehensile Tail:

Squirrel monkeys possess a long, non-prehensile tail that serves as a vital adaptation for their arboreal lifestyle. While not capable of grasping objects, the tail aids in balance and stability during rapid movements through the trees. It acts as a counterbalance, allowing for agile navigation in the complex canopy environment.

2. Grasping Hands and Feet:

Squirrel monkeys have opposable thumbs, allowing them to grasp and manipulate objects with precision. Their hands and feet are adapted for grasping tree branches, facilitating climbing and brachiation (swinging from branch to branch).

3. Strong Hind Limbs:

Their hind limbs are powerful and adapted for leaping and jumping. This agility is essential for navigating the three-dimensional space of the forest canopy. Squirrel monkeys can make remarkable leaps between branches, allowing them to cover large distances quickly.

10.1.2 Sensory Adaptations

1. Large Forward-Facing Eyes:

Squirrel monkeys have large, forward-facing eyes with well-developed depth perception. This adaptation is crucial for accurately judging distances while moving through the trees. The enhanced vision helps them detect predators and navigate their complex arboreal environment.

2. Excellent Color Vision:

These primates possess color vision, enabling them to distinguish a wide range of colors. This adaptation is useful for identifying ripe fruits, assessing the health of vegetation, and recognizing conspecifics based on facial and fur coloration.

10.1.3 Social and Behavioral Adaptations
1. Group Living:

Squirrel monkeys are highly social and live in multi-male, multi-female groups known as troops. Group living provides benefits such as increased vigilance against predators, cooperation in foraging, and social bonding. Their social structure involves complex relationships and hierarchical arrangements.

2. Communication Skills:

Vocalizations, facial expressions, and body language are integral components of squirrel monkey communication. They produce a variety of vocal sounds, including chirps, whistles, and chattering, to convey information within the group. This communication is crucial for coordinating group activities, alerting others to potential threats, and maintaining social bonds.

10.1.4 Dietary Adaptations

1. Omnivorous Diet:

Squirrel monkeys are opportunistic omnivores, consuming a diverse diet that includes fruits, insects, leaves, flowers, and small vertebrates. This dietary flexibility allows them to adapt to seasonal variations in food availability.

2. Foraging Techniques:

Their foraging behavior involves searching for food in the canopy. Squirrel monkeys use their grasping hands and agility to reach different parts of the trees. They may leap from branch to branch and even use their tails for balance while reaching for distant food sources.

10.1.5 Reproductive and Parental Adaptations
1. Seasonal Breeding:

Squirrel monkeys often exhibit seasonal breeding patterns, with reproduction linked to periods of increased food availability. This adaptation ensures that offspring are born during times when resources are more abundant.

2. Parental Care:

Both males and females in the troop contribute to the care of offspring. Parental care involves carrying, grooming, and protecting the young. This shared responsibility within the social group contributes to the well-being and survival of the offspring.

10.1.6 Thermoregulatory Adaptations
1. Limited Fur on Face:

Unlike some other primates, squirrel monkeys have limited fur on their faces. This adaptation may help dissipate heat more efficiently in their warm tropical environments, contributing to thermoregulation.

2. Behavioral Strategies for Temperature Regulation:
Squirrel monkeys engage in behavioral thermoregulation by seeking shade during the hottest parts of the day and adjusting their activity levels based on temperature. They may also engage in mutual grooming, which can help regulate body temperature.

Conclusion:
The unique adaptations of squirrel monkeys reflect their evolutionary history and specialization for life in the treetops of tropical rainforests. From prehensile tails and grasping hands to complex social structures and communication skills, these adaptations contribute to their success in navigating the challenges of their environment. Understanding these adaptations is essential for appreciating the ecological roles of squirrel monkeys and developing effective conservation strategies for their continued survival.

10.2 Cultural Significance

The cultural significance of squirrel monkeys spans various dimensions, incorporating both indigenous perspectives and broader cultural contexts. These primates, with their engaging behaviors and presence in tropical ecosystems, have captured the attention and interest of diverse communities. The cultural significance of squirrel monkeys can be explored through the following lenses:

10.2 Cultural Significance of Squirrel Monkeys
10.2.1 Indigenous Beliefs and Folklore
1. Symbolism in Indigenous Cultures:

In some indigenous cultures of South and Central America, animals, including squirrel monkeys, hold symbolic importance. They may be associated with specific spiritual beliefs, representing aspects of nature, fertility, or ancestral connections. The inclusion of these animals in folklore often reflects the intricate relationships between humans and the natural world.

2. Role in Creation Myths:

In certain indigenous myths and creation stories, animals like squirrel monkeys may play significant roles. These stories often emphasize the interconnectedness of all living beings and convey teachings about the balance of nature.

10.2.2 Wildlife Tourism and Conservation Awareness

1. Tourism Appeal:

Squirrel monkeys, with their lively behavior and distinctive appearance, contribute to the appeal of wildlife tourism in regions where they are found. Nature enthusiasts and tourists are drawn to observe these primates in their natural habitats, fostering a connection between people and the biodiversity of tropical ecosystems.

2. Conservation Symbol:

Squirrel monkeys can serve as charismatic ambassadors for wildlife conservation. Their presence in ecotourism initiatives and educational programs helps raise awareness about the importance of preserving natural habitats, biodiversity, and the delicate balance of ecosystems.

10.2.3 Educational and Scientific Value

1. Research Subjects:

Squirrel monkeys, including the Common Squirrel Monkey and other species, are subjects of scientific research in fields such as primatology, behavioral ecology, and conservation biology. Their cognitive abilities, social structures, and adaptations contribute valuable insights to our understanding of primate evolution and behavior.

2. Educational Outreach:

Squirrel monkeys featured in educational programs, documentaries, and zoological exhibits provide opportunities for the public to learn about the diversity of life on Earth. Educational outreach fosters an appreciation for biodiversity, the importance of conservation, and the interconnectedness of ecosystems.

10.2.4 Art, Literature, and Popular Culture
1. Artistic Representation:

Squirrel monkeys may be depicted in indigenous art, traditional crafts, and contemporary artistic expressions. Their unique appearance, vibrant fur patterns, and playful behaviors make them subjects of interest for artists and artisans.

2. Literary and Cultural References:

Squirrel monkeys, like many other animals, find their way into literature, folklore, and cultural expressions. Whether featured in children's stories or referenced in cultural metaphors, these primates become part of the cultural tapestry of the regions they inhabit.

3. Popular Culture:

In some instances, squirrel monkeys may find representation in popular culture, including films, advertisements, and media. Their engaging and curious nature can make them endearing characters in storytelling and entertainment.

Conclusion:

The cultural significance of squirrel monkeys extends beyond their ecological roles and scientific value. Indigenous beliefs, tourism, educational outreach, and artistic representations all contribute to the multifaceted cultural tapestry in which these primates are embedded. Understanding and appreciating the cultural significance of squirrel monkeys is essential for fostering conservation efforts, promoting biodiversity awareness, and recognizing the interconnected relationship between humans and the natural world.